DIG THOSE DINOSAURS

Lori Haskins Houran

Illustrated by Francisca Marquez

Albert Whitman & Company
Chicago, Illinois

Dig, dig, dig those dinosaurs
Dig, dig, dig those dinosaurs
Dig, dig, dig those dinosaurs

Dig those dinosaur bones.

So big, big, big those dinosaurs
Big, big, big those dinosaurs
Big, big, big those dinosaurs

Big, those dinosaur bones.

Jig, jig, jigsaw dinosaurs
Jig, jig, jigsaw dinosaurs
Jig, jig, jigsaw dino—

Oh!

Jigsaw dinosaur bones.

Rig, rig, rig those dinosaurs
Rig, rig, rig those dinosaurs
Rig, rig, rig those dinosaurs

Rig those dinosaur bones.

Dig, dig, dig those dinosaurs
Dig, dig, dig those dinosaurs
Dig, dig, dig those dinosaurs

DINOSAUR EXHIBIT

Dig those dinosaur bones!

Dig those dinosaurs

What do you need at a dinosaur dig? A shovel, of course. And…a *toothbrush*? Sometimes paleontologists—the scientists who search for dinosaur bones—use toothbrushes to clean dirt off bones. Another strange tool they use? Toilet paper! They wrap it around bones to cushion them.

So big, those dinosaurs

One of the biggest bones paleontologists have dug up so far is an *Argentinosaurus* bone that's five feet long and five feet wide. That one bone weighs more than 2,000 pounds! From head to tail, *Argentinosaurus* stretched 130 feet—longer than three school buses in a row.

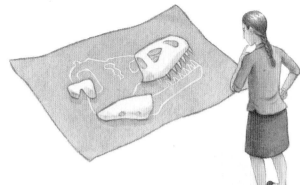

Jigsaw dinosaurs

It's not easy figuring out how dinosaur bones fit together. It's like putting together a puzzle…without the picture on the box! At first, scientists thought *Iguanodon's* thumb was part of its nose. And *Apatosaurus* was stuck with the skull of a completely different dinosaur! Even with all the bones in the right place, it's hard to tell how dinosaurs looked. Did they drag their tails behind them? Scientists used to think so, but now they believe dinosaurs held their tails up when they walked. We'll never know everything about dinosaurs, but with each new discovery, we learn more.

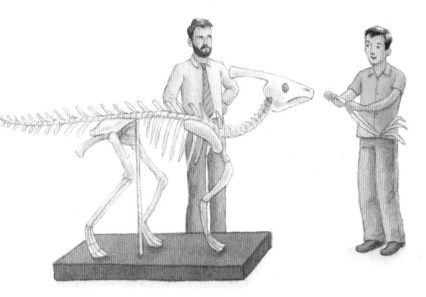

Rig those dinosaurs

Some dinosaur bones are over 200 *million* years old. So it's no surprise that they can be in rough shape. Before they go on display, broken bones are fixed with glue and plaster. Missing bones are replaced with dummies made of plastic or fiberglass.

Dig those dinosaur bones

The dinosaur bones paleontologists find are called fossils. Dinosaur eggs, footprints, and even droppings are fossils, too! The world's biggest collection of dinosaur fossils is at the American Museum of Natural History in New York City. More than half a million kids visit the museum every year.

For my guys, Jameson and Michael. I dig you! —LH

For my nephew, Aidan. —FM

Argentinosaurus-sized thanks to Carl Mehling at the American Museum of Natural History's Division of Paleontology for all his help with this book.

Library of Congress Cataloging-in-Publication Data
Houran, Lori.
Dig those dinosaurs / Lori Haskins Houran ;
illustrated by Francisca Marquez.
pages cm
ISBN 978-0-8075-1579-2 (hardcover)
1. Paleontology—Juvenile literature. I. Marquez, Francisca, illustrator.
II. Title.
QE714.5.H368 2013
567.9—dc23
2012017374

10 9 8 7 6 5 4 3 2 BP 17 16 15 14 13

The design is by Nick Tiemersma.

For more information about Albert Whitman & Company,
visit our web site at www.albertwhitman.com.